GUINNESS WORLD RECORDS

GUINNESS WORLD RECORDS

AMAZING SCHOOL RECORDS

KIDS WHO TEAMED UP FOR SUCCESS

Collect and Compare with

FEARLESS FEATS:
Incredible Records of Human Achievement

WILD LIVES:
Outrageous Animal & Nature Records

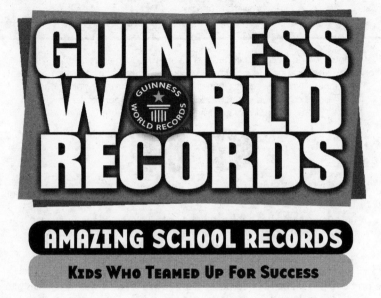

AMAZING SCHOOL RECORDS

KIDS WHO TEAMED UP FOR SUCCESS

Compiled by Ryan Herndon

For Guinness World Records: Laura Barrett, Craig Glenday,
Kim Lacey, Stuart Claxton, Betty Halvagi

SCHOLASTIC INC.

New York   Toronto   London   Auckland   Sydney
Mexico City   New Delhi   Hong Kong   Buenos Aires

Guinness World Records Limited has a very thorough accreditation system for records verification. However, while every effort is made to ensure accuracy, Guinness World Records Limited cannot be held responsible for any errors contained in this work. Feedback from our readers on any point of accuracy is always welcomed.

© 2005 Guinness World Records Limited, a HIT Entertainment Limited Company.

ISBN 0-439-80351-9

Designed by Rocco Melillo
Photo Research by Els Rijper
Records from the Archives of Guinness World Records

12 11 10 9 8 7 6 5 4 3 2 1   5 6 7 8 9 10/0

Printed in the U.S.A.

First printing, September 2005

Visit Scholastic.com for information about our books and authors online!
Visit Guiness World Records at www.guinessworldrecords.com

Contents

A lot of cool ideas got started in the United Kingdom—*Harry Potter*, putting meat and cheese between slices of bread and calling it a sandwich, and even the idea for *Guinness World Records*.

Not surprisingly, the idea grew out of a question. In 1951, Sir Hugh Beaver, the managing director of the Guinness Brewery, wanted to know which bird was faster—the golden plover or the grouse.

No one knew.

There wasn't even a book to settle the argument. But Sir Hugh found out that if anyone could answer his question, it would be the McWhirter twins.

Norris and Ross McWhirter were crazy about collecting information. They were just kids like you when they started clipping interesting facts from newspapers and memorizing important dates in world history. Later, they learned the names of every river and mountain range in the world, along with every nation's capital.

They never stopped collecting amazing and interesting facts, and after going to college, Norris and Ross started their own fact-finding business. They kept track of things like who held the record for pole-squatting (196 days in 1954) and which language had only one irregular verb (Turkish). They also knew that the grouse—flying at a speed of 43.5 miles per hour—is faster than the golden plover. They were the perfect people to compile the book that Sir Hugh wanted.

The first edition of *The Guinness Book of Records* was published on August 27, 1955, and since then has been published in 37 languages and in more than 100 countries. In its first fifty years it has sold more than 100 million copies, making it one of the best-selling books of all time!

Today, the official Keeper of the Records keeps a careful eye on each Guinness World Record, collecting and verifying the greatest the world has to offer—from the fastest to the slowest, the smallest to the tallest, and everything in between.

Introduction
Your School Did *What?*

For 50 years, *Guinness World Records* has been collecting cool facts about the world's most incredible record-breakers. Some records are silly. Some are serious. Some raise money for charity, and others simply raise spirits. In this collection, you'll discover some of the record-breaking accomplishments achieved by school kids and their teachers all over the world.

Whether these classmates built the biggest paper airplane ever, raced college students in the **LARGEST SACK RACE COMPETITION**, or created the **LARGEST HANDPRINT PAINTING** to earn new playground equipment for their school, real kids like you have set silly, serious, and spirit-raising world records.

These kinds of accomplishments mean one thing—teamwork. Students and teachers working together to achieve their goals made it all the way into the record book! We can accomplish a lot by doing our best in studies, sports, and setting records. But we truly achieve great things when we work together.

Remember that, and maybe one day someone will ask you, "Your school did *what?*" and you'll be on your way to a listing in *Guinness World Records*.

CHAPTER 1

Sticky Fingers

Sometimes all you need to do is lend a hand, or two, or 3,854! These students and teachers used their hands for planting, painting, puppeteering, and setting world records.

Read on to learn about the school that earned playground equipment with their handprints, and the students and teachers at eight schools who broke the record for **LARGEST SIGN LANGUAGE MASS PARTICIPATION** and learned a new way to talk to each other at the same time.

NAME OF SCHOOL: St. Therese's School

PLACE: Neath Port Talbot, UK

DATE: April 8, 2003

RECORD BROKEN: Most Trees Planted in an Hour

HOW THEY DID IT: The previous record of 3,500 trees planted by 100 people in Mexico was smashed on April 8, 2003 when a team of 96 students, parents, and teachers from St. Therese's School planted 4,100 trees during the 60-minute time limit. There were oak, hazel, hawthorn, beech, rowan, spindle, and horse chestnut trees, plus plenty of dirty hands and smiling faces.

WHY THEY DID IT: This was part of a plan to plant one tree for every child in the schools across the county. That's a tall order— more than 23,000 trees! But the county plans to keep on planting, and caring for the environment, for years to come.

Largest Amateur Puppet Show

NAME OF SCHOOL: Cockington Primary School

PLACE: Riviera International Centre, Torquay, Devon, UK

DATE: July 16, 2003

RECORD BROKEN: Largest Amateur Puppet Show

HOW THEY DID IT: Students ranging from 5 through 11 years old united to break this record! A total of 402 puppeteers handled 463 puppets in a production based on the Mayan myth of *Hurucan and the Feathered Snake.*

WHY THEY DID IT: Stage shows give students the chance to sing, dance, act, design sets and costumes, and even learn about puppetry! Onstage, kids use important skills such as listening, speaking, and working well with others to have a successful show.

Largest Sign Language
Mass Participation

NAME OF SCHOOL: Sweyne Park's Resource Base for Hearing Impaired Pupils, plus kids from seven other nearby schools

PLACE: Philip Morant School and College, Colchester, Essex, UK

DATE: October 8, 2004

RECORD BROKEN: Largest Sign Language Mass Participation

HOW THEY DID IT: Schools can unite in pursuit of a common goal—especially when that goal is record breaking. Eight schools participated in six months of planning for a mass demonstration during National Learn to Sign Week. A total of 1,927 participants broke the record. They signed the full alphabet under the watchful eyes of officials and teachers.

WHY THEY DID IT: The students felt a tremendous sense of pride and accomplishments in setting a new Guinness World Record and learning another way to communicate with one another.

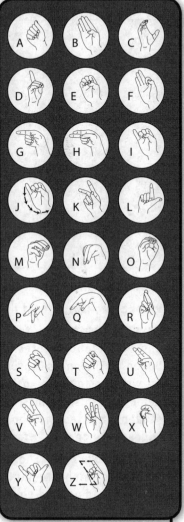

READING THE SIGNS

People who cannot hear or speak can communicate with others by reading lips or using their hands in a series of signals. The visual dictionary for these terms and symbols is called sign language. People who use sign language also use facial expressions to convey additional meanings in the same way hearing people use their voices to emphasize certain words in a conversation.

PLACE: Jeddah, Saudi Arabia **DATE:** November 15, 2002

RECORD BROKEN: Largest Handprint Painting

HOW THEY DID IT: Painted hands can reach across oceans to unite different cultures. Andrew David Forbes Henderson was the Queen of England's Consul General in Jeddah, Saudi Arabia, and his wife was a patron of the Star Givers charity. Together, they helped organize a massive art project in which 2,541 Saudi Arabian students coated their hands with paint to create the world's **LARGEST HANDPRINT PAINTING**.

WHY THEY DID IT: In England, Queen Elizabeth needed a special picture to celebrate her 50 years on the throne. In Saudi Arabia, a playground needed equipment for its many visitors. Her Majesty received a 2,251.76-square-foot painting of her official carriage, and the students earned their new playground equipment—and a world record!

SCHOOL: Unga Örnars Camp

PLACE: Fröjel, Gotland, Sweden

DATE: July 9, 2004

RECORD BROKEN: Longest Drawing

HOW THEY DID IT: In 1954, the United Nations recommended that all countries declare a Universal Children's Day to celebrate children. Activities are organized to promote the welfare of children around the world. A 9,251-foot-drawing, *My World*, was finished by 2,000 kids on Children's Day in

Batenburg Square, Sofia, Bulgaria, on June 1, 2003. It was the **LONGEST DRAWING** in the world—until July 9, 2004, when children at the Unga Örnars camp completed an even bigger drawing. Their masterpiece unrolled to the record-breaking length of 9,930 feet!

CHAPTER 2

Getting A's in Big Numbers

Wearing pajamas to school? Hugging a few—or 5,000—of your classmates? Check out these schools where teachers and students got together to break records in big numbers—*really big numbers*—and a family that set the record for perfect school attendance. Now *that's* teamwork.

PLACE: The McLean Bible Church and Dulles Town Center in Virginia, USA

DATE: February 1, 2003

RECORD BROKEN: Largest Sleepover/Pajama Party

HOW THEY DID IT: The perfect party requires planning. You need food, music, games, and lots of room if you are the host of the world's **LARGEST SLEEPOVER/PAJAMA PARTY**, which included 1,045 pajama-wearing students sacked out in sleeping bags. But that's not the only world record that involves sleepover games. On September 29, 2004, 2,773 participants in Dodgeville, Wisconsin, USA, swung their way to the record for **LARGEST PILLOW FIGHT**.

PJs in School?

Wearing pajamas is normally not allowed in schools. Yet some schools do organize special PJ Days in celebration of achieving classroom goals or to raise money for charity. In the USA, the National Education Association created a program named Read Across America in which the fun of reading is celebrated every day. Schools can plan contests and events, such as Dr. Seuss green-eggs-and-ham breakfasts and pajama reading parties with parents, to share the love of reading books with students (see photo). Talk with your teachers about any special-themed days planned for your class.

PLACE: Luohu District, Shenzhen City, China

DATE: September 20, 2003

RECORD BROKEN: Most People Brushing Their Teeth—Same Time, Same Place

HOW THEY DID IT: In China, the Chamber of Commerce and the Health and Education bureaus of the Luohu District organized a "mass brush-off" with thousands of kids wielding a mighty weapon: the toothbrush! Colgate-Palmolive (Guangzhou) Co. Ltd. sponsored the event as part of National Oral Health Day. Six dentists taught proper brushing technique to students standing in a line more than a half mile long. A total of 10,240 students brushed their teeth simultaneously to the tune of "You Brush, We All Brush" for at least 60 seconds. Their efforts scrubbed away plaque—and the old record!

Tooth Truths

The brush-off event in China was important because 76.55% of children there under the age of five have already suffered from tooth decay. We outgrow our baby teeth because our grown-up set is supposed to last the rest of our lives. Good dental hygiene keeps your teeth healthy and happy for a long time. Here are some tooth truths:

- Eat a balanced diet.

- Limit sweet treats that are high in sugar.

- Plaque is bacteria. Brushing and flossing will stop plaque from teaming up with sugars and acids to rot your teeth.

- Don't smoke! Smoking gives you bad breath, stains your teeth, and increases your risk of serious diseases.

- Set up a tooth routine: brush and floss at least twice a day.

- Fluoride in toothpaste and mouthwash strengthens developing teeth and helps prevent decay.

- Visit your dentist regularly.

SCHOOL: City Montessori School

PLACE: Lucknow, India

DATE: September 24, 2003

RECORD BROKEN: Largest School by Pupils

HOW THEY DID IT: Can you imagine how a school that opened with only five students in 1959 could enroll 27,911 pupils in 2003? This busy school beat its own world record of 26,312 students from the previous year! Boys and girls in India can start school as young as two years old and study through levels similar to those in an American high school. So students in the same school can be as young as 2 or as old as 18. The City Montessori School, founded by Jagdish and Bharti Gandhi, received the UNESCO Prize for Peace Education in 2002 for its leadership in organizing and hosting 15 international events for children each year.

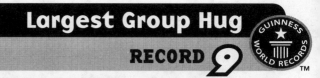

School: St. Matthew's Secondary School

Place: Orleans, Ontario, Canada

Date: April 23, 2004

Record Broken: Largest Group Hug

How They Did It: Not only did 5,117 students, staff, and friends break the record by hugging each other for a record-setting 10 seconds, they raised money for charity!

Why They Did It: A great day starts and ends with a hug. It's even more wonderful when your classmates, friends, and family huddle up for a group hug in the name of a good cause. This school teamed up with The Force, a local cancer charity, to raise money for the Ottawa Regional Cancer Center. They raised an incredible total of $106,000 for their group hug! What do you think everyone did after hearing the good news? Well, of course—they hugged each other again!

SCHOOL: Markethill County Primary and Markethill High School

PLACE: Armagh, Northern Ireland, UK

RECORD BROKEN: Longest School Attendance without Absences for a Family

HOW THEY DID IT: Perfect attendance is hard to achieve, except for the Stewart family! Seven sisters and brothers—Sharon, Neil, Honor, Howard, Olivia, Naomi, and Claire— finished their schooling from age 4 to 16 without being marked absent even once! The entire family earned the record for **LONGEST SCHOOL ATTENDANCE WITHOUT ABSENCES FOR A FAMILY**.

More gold stars went to 23 pupils of Ms. Melanie Murray during the academic year 1984–1985. The students formed the **LARGEST CLASS WITH MOST PERFECT ATTENDANCE** at David Barkley Elementary School in San Antonio, Texas, USA.

THE ISLE OF CHILDREN

Too many grown-ups crowding your world? Sail over to the Marshall Islands in the northern Pacific Ocean, where 39.1% of the population is under 15! This is the island home for the **LARGEST POPULATION OF CHILDREN**. In 2003, an estimated 22,063 of the 56,429 residents ranged in age from infant to 14 years old.

CHAPTER 3

Run, Jump, Dance Around

Could you leap your way to a world record? How about dance the Hokey Pokey? These schools danced, jumped, leaped, and raced their way into a Guinness World Record! Timing and teamwork were what it took to make sure these kids and teachers reached their goals.

Largest Sack Race Competition

RECORD 11

School: Agnieton College and several elementary schools in Zwolle, Wezep, and Hattern

Place: Zwolle, The Netherlands

Date: October 11, 2002

Record Broken: Largest Sack Race Competition

How They Did It: Being older doesn't always mean being better. Some bouncy elementary school kids in The Netherlands jumped into sacks and raced against college students to hop across the finish line first. A total of 2,095 students of mixed ages hopped into a world record! Curious about how fast one of these races can be? Ivanhoe Grammar School of Mernda, Victoria, in Australia, clocked in at 2 minutes 29.09 seconds for the **Fastest 4-x-100-meter Sack Relay Race** on June 17, 2003.

Largest Game of Leapfrog

RECORD 12

SCHOOL: Brookfield Community School

PLACE: Chesterfield, Derbyshire, UK

DATE: September 26, 2003

RECORD BROKEN: Largest Game of Leapfrog

HOW THEY DID IT: Have you ever played leapfrog— the game where your partner bends over and you leap over him or her like a frog? Then you stop, bend over, and your partner jumps over you. How would you like to have to leap over more than 800 people? A total of 849 students from

the Brookfield Community School leaped into the record book in the **LARGEST GAME OF LEAPFROG** ever. Timing, trust, and teamwork made this world record possible.

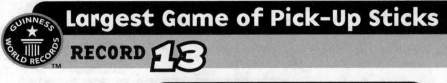
PLACE: Newmarket, New Hampshire, USA

DATE: July 21, 2003

RECORD BROKEN: Largest Game of Pick-up Sticks

HOW THEY DID IT: Have you ever played pick-up sticks? Easy, right? But what if those pick-up sticks were 36 times larger than the ones you can buy in the store? Four teams of 75 kids went to Newmarket, New Hampshire, to play a game and break the record for **LARGEST GAME OF PICK-UP STICKS**. Each stick measured 19 feet 10.5 inches long and 4.5 inches wide. Teams had to collect all 30 of their plastic sticks. That's exhausting work!

Largest Simultaneous Jump

RECORD 14

GUINNESS WORLD RECORDS™

PLACE: United Kingdom

DATE: September 7, 2001

RECORD BROKEN: Largest Simultaneous Jump

HOW THEY DID IT: Science Year started not with a bang, but with a jump! On September 7, 2001, a total of 569,069 kids and teachers from across the UK launched themselves into the air and kicked off the **LARGEST SIMULTANEOUS JUMP** precisely at 11:00 a.m. That number included 559,493 jumpers and more than 9,500 physically challenged students who dropped heavy objects or pounded the ground to simulate seismic activity. We don't know if the ground shook, but the old record toppled!

Largest Simultaneous
Hokey Pokey Dance

PLACE: Canada

DATE: April 9, 2002

RECORD BROKEN: Largest Simultaneous Hokey Pokey Dance

HOW THEY DID IT: The Foundation for Active Healthy Kids and the Canadian Association for Health, Physical Education, Recreation, and Dance coordinated the 681 participating schools for "activ8 the Nation's Schools Hokey Pokey Challenge." A total of 196,569 people across Canada put their right foot in a circle at the very same minute—11:15 a.m. CST. Eight minutes later, they finished shaking their way to a new world record!

WHY THEY DID IT: Canada danced on World Health Day to show that good health comes from staying active and having fun, especially at school!

Time to put your right foot out? You'll be doing the famous Hokey Pokey dance. This catchy tune started in the 1940s and became a dance craze for elementary school kids in the 1960s. Various songwriters claim to have created this simple, repetitive square dance. Participants form a circle and follow the song's silly instructions. By turning around several times and shaking various body parts, people always find their frowns turned into smiles. If you're feeling sad or angry, jump up and do the Hokey Pokey! You'll turn yourself around—and that's what life is all about!

CHAPTER 4

Sit on It

Check out the high school in Germany with 407 students and 1 chair, and the teacher in Poland who taught for more than 57 hours in a row! Whether they did it by riding unicycles, playing musical chairs, or sitting through the world's longest lesson, students just like you broke world records by sitting down!

NAME OF SCHOOL: Circus Jopie

PLACE: Utrecht, The Netherlands

DATE: May 18, 2003

RECORD BROKEN: Most People on Unicycles

HOW THEY DID IT: Have you ever wanted to join the circus? Well, you have to go to circus school first, even to be a clown! Circus clowns have a great sense of humor and *balance*. They often use unicycles in their acts and have learned how to fall safely. One hundred students from the Circus Jopie school traveled on individual unicycles for 1,150 feet. On their first try, the dragon costume that the students wore was 1,475 feet long and split in two! Their second attempt, without the costume, was a success.

UNICYCLES are bikes with only one wheel and a seat. No handlebars, it's just you and a good sense of balance.

**EXPERT TIPS FOR
NEW UNICYCLE RIDERS:**

- Gear up with a helmet and wrist pads.

- Average learning curve: about 10–15 hours, or practice an hour every day for two weeks.

- Check the foot pedals marked L for left and R for right.

- Adjust the seat until your leg is almost straight. Your foot should be on the pedal at its lowest point.

- Practice on softer ground, not on concrete. A fence or handrail is necessary for balancing until you're ready to let go. Think safety first!

- Although you're the only one on the bike, there are clubs for unicyclists who want to pedal together.

NAME OF SCHOOL: Otto-Hahn-Gymnasium

PLACE: Springe, Germany

DATE: September 20, 2002

RECORD BROKEN: Most People Sitting on One Chair

HOW THEY DID IT: Imagine being in a classroom with just one chair. High school students in Germany organized a single-chair sit-down to set a new record. The call went out for 407 kids, plus 1 chair. How did all of those students manage this daring feat? Each student sat down on the knees of the classmate right behind them to form an unbroken line 199 feet 1.2 inches long!

NAME OF SCHOOL: Anglo-Chinese School

PLACE: Singapore

DATE: August 5, 1989

RECORD BROKEN: Largest Game of Musical Chairs

HOW THEY DID IT: The **LARGEST GAME OF MUSICAL CHAIRS** kicked off with 8,238 students. The music played and stopped and played and stopped and played...for three hours and thirty minutes! When the music stopped for the last time, only 15-year-old Xu Chong Wei was left sitting. Good thing this school wasn't trying for the chair-sitting record—ouch! No doubt you've played musical chairs at birthday parties, too. Players walk in a circle around chairs, listening to music. Everybody scrambles for a seat when the music stops. The catch? There aren't enough chairs. One person is eliminated in each round, until there's just one person left sitting—the winner!

NAME OF SCHOOL: Sutherland Library

PLACE: Sydney, New South Wales, Australia

DATE: May 24 to May 27, 2004

RECORD BROKEN: Longest Reading-Aloud Marathon by a Team

HOW THEY DID IT: We all know how much fun reading, and being read to, can be. Who better to do the reading than people who love books, like librarians? Local librarians from Sydney, Australia, read to a group gathered inside the Sutherland Library for 81 hours and 15 minutes. Let's hope they had comfortable chairs!

WHY THEY DID IT: The librarians organized the event to celebrate Australian Library week and to raise money for local charities.

NAME OF SCHOOL: Liceum Ogólnoksztalcace

PLACE: Poznan, Poland

DATE: February 15 to 17, 2003

RECORD BROKEN: Longest Lesson

HOW THEY DID IT: Does it sometimes feel like the bell will *never* ring? Imagine how Marek Gubanski's students felt when their class-ending bell finally rang after 57 hours and 30 minutes. Teacher Gubanski taught theater, literature, film, language, and Polish culture to 20 very patient students in order to break a world record.

CHAPTER 5

Classroom Construction

These students teamed up to build things like the world's largest yo-yo, the biggest DNA model, and the longest LEGO® structure ever. They used various materials, from paper to plastic to rubber chickens, but there was one thing all these students had in common—another kid's help!

Place: Potteries Shopping Centre, Stoke-on-Trent; and Earl's Court, London, UK

Date: March 9 through July 10, 2002

Record Broken: Largest Model of DNA

How They Did It: The genetic code of life curls inside the cells of each human being. Deoxyribonucleic acid, or DNA for short, forms long molecules or strands shaped like twisted rope ladders of chemical building blocks. More than 3,000 British school kids teamed up with scientists and other adults to build a 40-foot tall model of DNA. They started work at Potteries Shopping Centre in Stoke-on-Trent, UK, and finished the monster model at Earl's Court in London.

NAME OF SCHOOL:
Stockport College

PLACE: Greater Manchester, UK

DATE: August 1, 1993

RECORD BROKEN:
Largest Yo-Yo

HOW THEY DID IT:
Supposedly, the yo-yo got its name in the 1910s from the Filipino word meaning

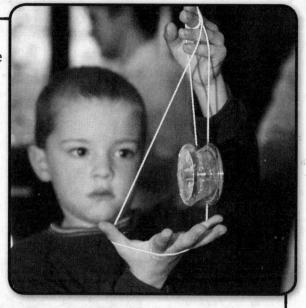

"to return." Students tested out this theory by building a giant working model. J. N. Nichols from the British soft drink company, Vimto Ltd., designed it, and the students built it. At 896 pounds and with a diameter of 10 feet 4 inches, this mammoth yo-yo required a crane to lift and drop it from a height of 188 feet 7 inches. Like all good yo-yos should, it did return, slowly, four different times on August 1, 1993!

WHY THEY DID IT: Kids have had fun with yo-yos for centuries! Archeologists found clay yo-yos among 2,500-year-old Greek relics. French leader Napoleon Bonaparte relaxed, and practiced eye-hand coordination, by using a yo-yo. In 1985, the first toy to go into and return from orbit aboard the space shuttle was—you guessed it—the yo-yo.

Largest Flying Paper Airplane Built

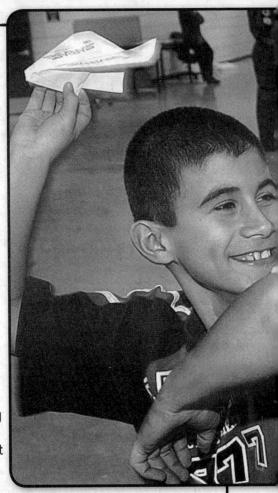

NAME OF SCHOOL: Delft University of Technology

PLACE: Delft, The Netherlands

DATE: May 16, 1995

RECORD BROKEN: Largest Paper Airplane Built

HOW THEY DID IT: Some aerospace engineers start working on their flight skills at early ages. A team of aerospace engineering students constructed the **LARGEST FLYING PAPER AIRPLANE BUILT** ever. Its wingspan was 45 feet 10 inches, about the width of a basketball court. Would a paper airplane that big actually fly? This one did. Its successful flight covered a distance of 114 feet 2 inches!

WHY THEY DID IT: Paper construction is one of the oldest and most basic art forms. We don't all practice *origami*, the intricate and delicate Japanese art of folding paper, but everyone has made a paper airplane at least once.

LINK UP

Organization is the key to building any structure. Practice your building skills using simple materials, such as construction paper. An easy and fun project is to make a chain of colorful paper links.

TIPS FROM RECORD SETTERS:

- Get supplies early.
- Clear out a big workspace.
- Ask friends to handle the food, drinks, and music during the event while you and your team get organized.

The **LONGEST PAPER CHAIN** was made by 60 people in 24 hours at Alvin Community College in Alvin, Texas, USA, on October 23–24, 1998. It consisted of 584,000 links and measured 51.8 *miles* long!

PLACE: Montreal, Quebec, Canada

DATE: April 15, 2004

RECORD BROKEN: Longest LEGO® Structure

HOW THEY DID IT: Future architects of the world practice their skills at a young age by using building blocks. The popular plastic construction toy LEGO® is ideal for making big, multicolored, and multishaped structures. Worldwide competitions take place using LEGO® pieces to create the largest structures, though not all of the blocks are little. The record holder is a millipede-shaped structure that measured 4,586 feet 6 inches long. More than 20,000 children in Montreal, Quebec, Canada, snapped together the 3,000,000 bricks.

Largest Rube Goldberg Machine

GUINNESS WORLD RECORDS™

NAME OF SCHOOL: Monache High School

PLACE: Porterville, California, USA   **DATE:** January through July, 1997

RECORD BROKEN: Largest Rube Goldberg Machine

HOW THEY DID IT: The term "Rube Goldberg" means doing something very simple in an unnecessarily complicated and intricate way. Constructing a Rube Goldberg machine is a great way for students to study the cause-and-effect process. The ultimate result may be simple, like a machine that waves a flag or inserts batteries. The challenge lies in creating as many steps as possible to bring about that simple result. The record holders for constructing the **LARGEST RUBE GOLDBERG MACHINE** are a team of twelve students who built a machine that gave change for 50 cents. To make change, you inserted two quarters into the machine. After a total of *113 more steps*—including flushing a toilet, and making a doll's head and a rubber chicken move—you received 50 pennies!

CHAPTER 6

Get Together

Some record attempts raise money for charity. Others raise spirits by making people laugh. Check out these records in which kids like you raised their voices, earned money for charity, and made people laugh when they came together to break world records.

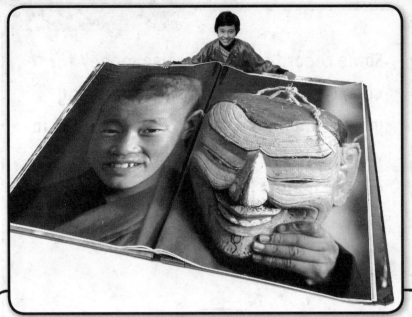

NAME OF SCHOOL: Massachusetts Institute of Technology (MIT)

PLACE: New York, USA

DATE: December 15, 2003

RECORD BROKEN: Largest Published Book

HOW THEY DID IT: Many people dream of writing and publishing their own book someday. In most dreams, the book fits on a bookshelf. A book far too large for any shelf was created by students working with, and learning from, experienced book publishers and printers. MIT provided the students, while Acme Bookbinding and Friendly Planet offered the know-how and materials. When the teams unveiled their full color book, *Bhutan*, in New York, the **LARGEST PUBLISHED BOOK** weighed 133 pounds, stood 5 feet high, and spanned 7 feet when opened.

Largest Human Centipede

RECORD 27

GUINNESS WORLD RECORDS™

NAME OF SCHOOL: Nagoya Otani High School

PLACE: Tsuruma Track and Field Stadium, Japan

DATE: June 13, 2001

RECORD BROKEN: Largest Human Centipede

HOW THEY DID IT: A centipede is a fast-moving insect with a long, slender body that is divided into several segments, usually with one pair of legs on each segment. While this bug can move quickly, humans trying to imitate centipedes need to move carefully at a much slower pace...or they'll fall over! Students, parents, and teachers—a total of 2,026 people—moved together for 98 feet 6 inches—without any missteps. Challengers in Hong Kong made a record attempt with their feet tied to the person next to them... all 684 of them. Better luck next time!

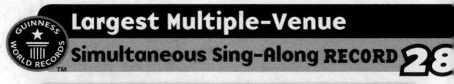

Largest Multiple-Venue
Simultaneous Sing-Along RECORD 28

PLACE: United Kingdom

DATE: December 9, 2002

RECORD BROKEN: Largest Multiple-Venue Simultaneous Sing-Along

HOW THEY DID IT: A 10-year-old singer named Declan Galbraith was joined by a total of 83,637 voices from choirs in hundreds of schools across the UK at precisely 2:45 p.m. for the **LARGEST MULTIPLE-VENUE SIMULTANEOUS SING-ALONG**. They had practiced a special song, "Tell Me Why," written for this record-breaking performance.

WHY THEY DID IT: These pitch-perfect choirs raised their voices to raise money to help find the cure for cancer. The Young Voices Choir, Sargent Cancer Care of Children, and the recording management company EMI organized the event.

Most Basketballs Dribbled
Simultaneously RECORD 29

NAME OF SCHOOL:
Serpell Primary
School

PLACE: Templestowe,
Victoria, Australia

DATE: October 15,
2004

RECORD BROKEN: Most
Basketballs Dribbled
Simultaneously

HOW THEY DID IT:
A total of 847
students gathered
together to show
their basketball
skills and to break
a world record.
This group bounced
the old record by
staying in one spot
for a minimum of 5
minutes while each
of the 847 students each dribbled a basketball!

Most People Wearing Groucho Marx
Glasses—Same Place, Same Time

NAME OF SCHOOL: East Lansing High School

PLACE: East Lansing, Michigan, USA

DATE: May 23, 2003

RECORD BROKEN: Most People Wearing Groucho Marx Glasses—Same Place, Same Time

HOW THEY DID IT: There is a simple rule in comedy: Disguises are funny. Groucho Marx was a famous vaudeville comedian known for his recognizable face and mannerisms. He wore thick black glasses beneath his bushy eyebrows and sported a short mustache under his rather large nose.

His face was so unique that it became the perfect face for mask makers to model zany disguises. The popularity of wearing a Groucho Marx disguise sprang out of his movie *Duck Soup*, because two of his brothers, Harpo and Chico, dressed up and acted like him during several scenes.

Months of planning with school administration, teachers, and students culminated in a record and the biggest laugh ever, when eight hundred people donned the funny disguise and managed to stay in one place with the mask on their face for 20 minutes.

WHY THEY DID IT: Joe Kavanagh, a sophomore with a dream to set a Guinness World Record with his classmates, started it all. Sometimes all it takes is one kid—just like you—to bring people together and set a record attempt in motion.

Be a Record-Breaker!

MESSAGE FROM THE OFFICIAL KEEPER OF THE RECORDS:

Record breakers are the ultimate in one way or another—the youngest, the oldest, the tallest, the smallest. So how do you get to be a record-breaker? Follow these important steps:

1. Before you attempt your record, check with us to make sure your record is suitable and safe. Get your parents' permission. Next, contact one of our officials by using the record application form at *www.guinnessworldrecords.com.*

2. Tell us about your idea. Give us as much information as you can, including what the record is, when you want to attempt it, where you'll be doing it, and so on.

   a) We will tell you if a record already exists, what safety guidelines you must follow during your attempt to break that record, and what evidence we need as proof that you have completed your attempt.

   b) If your idea is for a brand-new record nobody has set yet, we need to make sure it meets our requirements. If it does, then we'll write official rules and safety guidelines specific to that record idea and make sure all attempts are made in the same way.

3. Whether it is a new or existing record, we will send you the guidelines for your selected record. Once you receive these, you can make your attempt at any time. You do not need a Guinness World Record official at your attempt. But you do need to gather evidence. Find out more about the kind of evidence we need to see by visiting our website.

4. Think you've already set or broken a record? Put all of your evidence as specified by the guidelines in an envelope and mail it to us at Guinness World Records, 338 Euston Road, London NW1 3BD.

5. Our officials will investigate your claim fully—a process that can take up to 10 weeks, depending on the number of claims we've received, and how complex your record is.

6. If you're successful, you will receive an official certificate that says you are now a Guinness World Record holder!

Need more info? Check out the Kids' Zone on *www.guinnessworldrecords.com* for lots more hints and tips and some top record ideas that you can try at home or at school. Good luck!

See what **you can do** if you **work together**?!

Guinness World Records is all about recognizing the best records around the world. We know that many record breakers are just like you – at school! That's why our 2006 book has pages specially designed for what you will like, such as **young record breakers**, **computer games**, and the **X Games**.

It's important for you and your friends to have fun with *Guinness World Records*. This is why we are including – for the first time ever – **exclusive trading cards** in the 2006 book. They are the first eight in a set of 120 that will come out this year, and they will show you the fun you can have while collecting – or trading with your friends.

Photo Credits

The publisher would like to thank the following for their kind permission to use their photographs in this book: